7 Secrets to
Surviving College

The Gardner family,

keep thriving in society
wo need more families to
show us how its done!

11 / 1 / 2018

(419) 984-2282

insta: Chrisscott motivates

reach to teach national @gmail.com

7 Secrets to Surviving College

Christopher C. Scott, M.Ed.

To order additional copies of this book, contact:
Xlibris
1-888-795-4274
www.Xlibris.com
Orders@Xlibris.com
770773

Contents

Introduction iii

Dedication.. 1

Chapter 1: Passion Over Paper 5

Chapter 2: Sacrifices.. 17

Chapter 3: Control Your Inner Hater............................. 33

Chapter 4: Get Some Positive Friends 45

Chapter 5: The Power of the GPA 55

Chapter 6: Adjust Your Mind-Set 67

Chapter 7: Take No Losses!...75

INTRODUCTION

F IRST, I WOULD like to thank you for purchasing my book. Whether you are simply thinking about college or are in the process of returning from a hiatus, the material that we cover in this book will provide you with key steps to achieving success throughout your college career. This book focuses on sharing valuable information on surviving college along with real-life experiences both from my college journey and the journeys of other students. The truth of these stories and the resulting tips are sure to be felt by many youth today, especially those who hail from the inner city.

You may be wondering what inspired me to write this book. The answer to this is not a simple one. Being the first in my family to attend college was very difficult. I did not know what to prepare for or who to look to when I needed support. My lack of knowledge and direction lead me to take note on what I believed to be some of the most valuable tips for an incoming freshman. Tips that I wish someone had shared with me as a fresh college student. It took me a lot of time to analyze the hidden messages between the obstacles that I faced throughout my undergraduate years. Although I love speaking about college survival, I know that I will someday grow old, and the new students of upcoming generations will no longer trust the words of an "old man." Writing this book gives me an opportunity to reach prospective and current college students, regardless of my age. This book also provides those students with vital information that's not often found in textbooks or shared by mentors.

Ultimately, this book is designed to help college students add focus to their college journey. One of my main goals was to ensure this material was a short yet entertaining read, as I know many students will receive a lot of mandatory reading materials from their academic classes. Students can feel free to pick up this book whenever they are seeking some quick guidance or in need of a laugh throughout the day. Staying true to my goofy personality I was sure to incorporate a bit of humor throughout this book.

Please share these secrets with others, as these ideas may help them successfully navigate college. Again, thank you for reading. I truly hope you enjoy it!

DEDICATION

I DEDICATE THIS book to my family and my extended network of family and friends. You all have helped influence my thinking process. I know I have changed for the better.

To my hilarious mother, Everetta Brown. This woman has the heart of a lion. She spent most of her life raising me and my six siblings, mostly on her own. I'm very thankful that you decided to keep us all, even though you probably wanted to leave us on a church doorstep somewhere (LOL!). I'm forever thankful. I'm very proud of what you have accomplished thus far; keep pushing, Momma!

To my four big brothers. Terrell Brown, although I didn't see you much as a child, it was always fun watching you come to the house. You were like a celebrity to us. Darrell Brown, the goofiest brother that I have. I believe I get most of my silly ways from you. Darnell Brown, the most creative brother in the house. I remember watching you build three-dimensional cars out of popsicle sticks. You opened up the world of creativity for me. Johnny Scott, my dark-skin twin, the bodybuilder and computer guru in the family, I'm not sure when you started working out, but you have always been my inspiration to start weight-training. I've got to keep up with you.

To my two younger sisters, Tenesha Scott and Mattretta Mathews. As a child, I know I annoyed the crap out of you. I've been in trouble with my mother so many times for bugging my oldest sister, Tenesha. For whatever reason, I managed to sneak under my mother's radar when it came to the youngest, Mattretta. This doesn't mean that these two didn't have their own ways of dealing with me. To this day, I still have bruises on my body from their ferocious bear attacks.

I'd like to dedicate this book to my best friend and guardian angel, my Wife Mrs. Shawnterra Scott. I honestly don't know where I would be if we had not crossed paths in life. They say God places people in your life for a reason. I can honestly say He had a plan putting us together. We have seen each other cry over, struggle with, and smile at just about everything under the sun. When my motivation was down, you always brought me back up. You truly are an angel, Shawnterra.

Finally, I want to extend special thanks to all of my social media support base. Surprised to see yourselves in my dedication? Don't be. We connect on various different levels through our daily posts and interactions. I'm honored that you take the time to read my posts and take many of my messages home with you. Please stay in touch—let's continue to grow and learn together.

CHAPTER 1

Passion Over Paper

BEING THE FIRST in my family to go off to college was a very interesting yet scary adventure. My parents didn't know much about what I should expect in college, because neither of them had been there. I had my mind made up that I would pursue a career in pharmaceutical science, because I was told that's where the "big bucks" were. I'll never forget my first college classroom experience. I remember walking into this huge lecture hall classroom—the type that seats about 200 to 300 students. It was the kind of classroom that I had only seen in movies that depicted college.

Being a new student, I tried to find the seat where I would feel most comfortable. I found the perfect movie theater seat. You know, the seat where you aren't too close to the screen, nor are you too far back. You're right in the middle of the classroom, where your neck isn't tilted so far back that it's breaking just to look at the screen. I remember thinking, "Wow! This is interesting—my first college class!" I was excited but a bit nervous all at the same time. My first class of the day was a chemistry lecture. I wasn't a huge fan of chemistry, but I was ready for whatever the professor was about to teach us, or so I thought. I had my chemistry book, notebook, pens, and pencils, so to me, I was ready to go! Ten minutes into the class, the other students and I all began to wonder whether the professor was even coming. Suddenly, the class went very quiet. All of our eyes began to focus on the older gentleman who had walked in from a hidden door. He was a white older male, in about his sixties, with a serious potbelly. He truly looked like good ol' Saint Nick—a real-life Santa Claus. He had a meter stick in his hand with a candle attached to it, and for whatever reason, he began to light the candle.

At this time, he hadn't said anything to us yet. We didn't know whether this man was the professor or some lunatic trying to set us on fire! Suddenly, two more individuals appeared from that same door, both carrying red balloons. They set the balloons down in front of the classroom and exited silently. The older gentleman looked at the class, and without saying a word, raised his burning meter stick and lit the balloons on fire. Both balloons went up in flames without any noticeable difference between them. The older gentleman looked back at us and said, "Okay, students, I need you to tell me what was inside those balloons. Once you figure that out, I need you to write an equation explaining what just happened. Once that is complete, I need you to balance the equation. You have five minutes."

WTH WAS THAT!?

My face and response to the professor's questions

I began to sweat so hard I literally felt my armpits destroying my deodorant! I thought to myself, is this man serious right now? I was expecting him to at least introduce himself to us first. Something along the lines of, "Hi, students, my name is Professor Claus. I'm excited to be teaching you chemistry this year. Please stand up and introduce yourselves." I came to class that day expecting to introduce myself, sharing where I'm from and a fun fact about myself, but this man went straight for the kill! I sat there clueless. Hell, I didn't know what was inside those balloons, and I couldn't begin to imagine what kind of equation he wanted! So, I sat there sweating bullets. I looked over to my neighbor on the left to see whether he could help me get started. He was sitting there with the same "I don't know what to do!" look as well. But the guy to my right was hard at work figuring out what to write down. He seemed intrigued and focused on answering questions that seemed impossible to me.

It took me two years to figure out what this professor was trying to do that day. My mind was always puzzled, wondering why a professor would frighten us on the first day of classes. He knew that we were freshman students. I'm sure he knew that we were nervous about being in our first college class. Why would he scare us like that? Here's what I came up with. Studying in any science-based field is a true challenge, and any degree you receive will hold great importance but will also require you to exercise great responsibility. The sciences are a big deal. Students who finish these programs often make a highly gainful living upon graduation and usually are gainfully employed throughout their professional years. Salaries start at $80,000 per year and can exceed $200,000. I realized that this professor was trying to teach us something that day. He was trying to "weed out" the students in who were solely focused on making the big money that comes at the end of the road of a science-based program–to separate them from the students who were actually interested in the content. And, let me tell you, he weeded me out of that classroom faster than you can imagine. The moment that class ended, I immediately requested to switched to a lower-level chemistry course!

So, here is the first secret to surviving college. When it comes to choosing your major and career, go into something that you are either passionate about or something that you are good at. Again, choose something that you are **passionate** about, or something that you are **good** at. I share this first because this is going to be the glue that helps you stick to college. If you're going into a program solely based on the money, like I did as a freshman, you could be setting yourself up for failure.

Me praying you make the right choice for you

Choosing a major based on salary could cause you to start college with an unstable foundation, because you won't have any real interest in the material that you're learning. This lack, or underdeveloped, interest in your area of study has the potential to act as a barrier to success. Remember the student sitting on my right in class who was intrigued by the questions presented by the professor. He was ready to embrace the challenge. That student was either passionate about the material he was being exposed to or he was good at it. It's best when you, as a student, have **both** of those qualities.

Personally, I had no real interest in the pharmacy program. I was told in high school that my dream of being an educator wouldn't allow me to make any money. Many teachers said that I should go into pharmacy to make a lot of money. I do recall one teacher telling me that being a pharmacist wouldn't fit my personality. She pointed out that I'm a person who likes to talk and interact with people, and because of that, I shouldn't consider pharmacy. That was my science teacher, Ms. Braun, and she was right!

I knew before coming to college that I was an educator at heart, whether it's educating in the classroom setting, giving a motivational presentation, or teaching others through this book. I knew that educating was something I'm both **passionate** about and something I believe I'm personally **good** at–and my overall experience in college changed for the better because I followed this self-imposed rule. My freshman year, I decided to stay in the pharmacy program with the belief that maybe it would get better, that someday I would grow to become passionate about and good at this content. Well, my freshman grades didn't tell that same narrative. My cumulative GPA at the end of my first year was a 2.7. It was difficult for me to internalize how horribly I had done my freshman year. I wish I had switched my major earlier.

The second year, I transferred into the college of education. Again, this is an area I'm passionate about and also something I'm good at. Sure enough, my GPA for the first semester after switching to education rose to a 3.5, bringing my cumulative GPA up to comfortable 3.0. Reading this, you might be happy for me (I hope), but you're also probably wondering, "how do **you** figure out what **your** passions are or what you're good at?" Being passionate about something is a bit complicated to explain. I typically tell students that your passion is probably the thing that you can see yourself doing for free. It's also a subject that makes you happy. I'm not saying that you should work for free, but if money weren't a concern, what would you do? That's probably your passion. I love to educate, and there have been many times that I have spoken for free. Ultimately, I speak to groups because it makes me happy, but I can also get paid to speak.

When it comes to deciding what you are good at, I'm referring to your academic strengths. Some students are really good at math and science. If those are subjects that you thrive in, then get involved in a college program that's heavy in those subject areas.

If you know you do really well in art, further your education in the arts. Some people may still tell you to go into an area where you will get paid a great deal of money. I personally say, do what makes you happy. I'm a firm believer that if you are passionate about or really good at your craft, and others can see your passion and your talent, they will pay you to continue to do what you are passionate about.

<u>Student-to-Student Tip #1:</u>

Don't be afraid to introduce yourself to the professor.

Going to college can be a scary journey. If you get a professor like mine the first time around, make sure you're wearing really good deodorant! In all seriousness, your professors are human, and they want to see you succeed in class because this makes them look good to their superiors. Sometimes knowing your professors can make all the difference in your college journey. One of your professors might end up being your mentor, or you may need a professor to write a letter of recommendation on your behalf someday. Sometimes knowing the professor can even have positive effects on the grade you receive in that class!

A Time to Reflect

1. How are you feeling about going to college? Are you excited? If so, what are you excited about? If you are nervous, what's making you feel that way?

2. Throughout the chapter, college major and career choice is discussed. Do you agree or disagree with the idea of choosing your passion over money?

3. What are you passionate about?

4. Do you believe I made a wise decision when I decided to change my major?

<u>**Scholarship Hunt Tip #1:**</u>

Check with your high school's faculty and staff for student scholarships offered by your high school's Alumni Association, if they have one. When I was in high school I was not aware of what an alumni association was. I had seen and heard about my high school's alumni association in the community and around school but I was unaware of who they were. I was also unaware of their purpose. After discovering my high school's alumni chapter, I'd found that they offer yearly scholarships to graduation seniors. I received a $6500.00 from my high school's alumni associate. This money was paid directly to my first year college fees! So my advice is to check with your high school's alumni association. You could receive some additional money to cover school expenses.

CHAPTER 2

Sacrifices

TO SUCCEED IN college, one of the key things that you will need to do is to make some serious sacrifices. So here you have it: secret number two to surviving and thriving in college is sacrificing [drum roll]…

YOUR CELL PHONE!

Now what do I mean when I say sacrifice your cell phone? I don't mean throw the phone against the wall and break it or cast your phone into a fire pit! However, you do have to be willing to put your phone away so you can focus in class.

Let's do a quick role-playing example. Imagine we are both in an 8 a.m. lecture. Physically you are in class, but mentally you are back in your bedroom still asleep, because it is 8 a.m. DAMN IT! Suddenly, your phone begins to sound off in your pocket. Now, if you are like any other human being, you'll be curious about who else is up at 8 a.m. and why they're messaging you. This urge will be especially strong if your lecture is on a topic that holds little interest.

Class topic holding little interest

So here's what you are going to do. You're going to pull your phone out of your pocket, look at the tweet or text message, smile, and tweet or text back. The next thing you know, you are going to take a look at the professor, look at the time, and notice you are no closer to getting out of that lecture. Not only will you see that no time has passed, but in that short minute, the professor has moved on to a totally different topic.

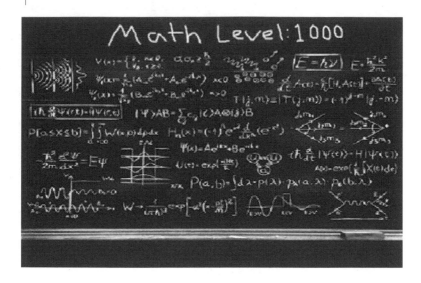

Class topic you just missed in one minute

Now you're lost. This will cause you to mentally check out of the lecture, because your entire learning flow has been compromised.

I always tell students, take your cell phone and put that thing on silent, not vibrate. There is a big difference. When your phone is on vibrate, it's just as bad as the phone sounding off in your pocket. It's still going to pull your attention away from the lecture. Now, some of you reading this book may say, "Okay, Chris, you got me! I'll put my phone on silent so it doesn't distract me in class, sheesh!"

So now your phone is on silent. But this means nothing and does not help you at all if you're going to leave it on your desk like this:

Your phone(s) are facing up, this will distract you!

That isn't going to work either! Once your phone lights up with texts and notifications, it's going to break your focus, just as a ring or a vibration would.

You say, "Okay, Chris! You got me again, this time I will put my phone on silent, not vibrate, and I will flip it so I cannot see the screen. Now I can't see or hear the phone when it goes off. Is this good enough? Does this suffice as my cell phone sacrifice?" Well, reader, it depends. Following these two steps—silencing your phone instead of leaving it on vibrate, and placing it face down on your desk—are great starts for MOST students. For MOST students, this might actually help them stay focused in class.

But there's a special kind of student who's still out there. These students use a different method to help them see when someone is calling or texting their phone. If you are the student who flips the phone on its back so you can't see the screen but your phone's flash illuminates when a text alert comes to your phone, you need to put your phone completely out of sight to maintain your focus in class. I know you probably weren't expecting me to think about that, but hey, I'm just trying to help you focus in class! My freshman year, I didn't know how important sacrificing my cell phone during class was. Sometimes I wish someone had told me. There were many times in classroom lectures where I got lost in my phone playing *Angry Birds* (which was new at the time) or checking my Facebook account (Twitter was not yet popular, and Instagram and Snapchat weren't yet invented).

Now, the need to sacrifice your cell phone might not be a survival requirement for everyone. Some of us reading this book might have different distractions that could get in the way of our college education. Some of us might be chronic gamers who may need to cut back on the time we spend playing video games before and after class. Some reading this book may spend too much time watching television and may have to cut back. There will also be some of you chronic party animals who may have to leave the jungle! Whatever your challenge may be, if it negatively affects your performance and focus in the classroom or during study times, it might be best to consider cutting back on that activity so you can be more successful in your academics. Note that sacrificing doesn't necessarily mean that you have to give up your distraction completely; just make adjustments on the time you spend for leisure to see improvement in the classroom.

Along with sacrificing your cell phone, there are some other things that you may have to give up in college to be successful. This is where the talk gets realer than real...

You may find that you have to sacrifice some PEOPLE so that you can be successful in college. And, in some cases, it might be the people that you consider to be your "besties" or "day ones." Some of us reading this book have besties and day ones who don't act like the supportive lifelong friends they claim to be. I don't know why we even give them the "friend" title if they don't support positivity and growth. You will find that some people will be more detrimental to you, rather than supportive of your success. In some cases, these people may even be your family. This can be rare, but yes, it happens.

I'll share this story about a young man from the inner city of Cleveland who came to campus for orientation as an incoming student. The idea behind campus orientation is to connect incoming students with the final information and resources they need to be prepared for their first semester of classes. This is the day where prospective students receive their student IDs, get their class schedules, and meet some fellow incoming freshmen. In short, this is supposed to be one of the happiest days for an incoming college student: the final step before officially beginning college. While this should be the best day ever, for one student I saw, that was not the case. I witnessed a parent extensively badgering their child at 8 a.m., just before the orientation program began. "I can't believe you done dragged me all the way from Cleveland to go to this expensive-ass school! You don't have to come here for college! Go to the community college; it's right down the street! Who's going to pay for all this shit? Who's going to help me with your little sister and brother back at home? Who's going to help me with these bills that I need help with? Ain't nobody got time for this shit!" Now, this mother's rant was much longer than what I wrote. There were plenty more of those "$#@$%" symbols flying out of her mouth. But the most disturbing and embarrassing part of it all was that she was doing this in front of everyone. It was almost as if the world paused and focused only on this mother and her son. My colleagues and I stood to the side of the auditorium stunned.

WAIT...

WHY SHE DOING THAT?

Colleagues and I in shock!

The orientation program proceeded as usual, and after the main welcome, students sat down to meet with their academic advisors and review their class schedules for the upcoming semester. The advisors welcomed all the students and began to hand out their class schedules. When this young guy received his schedule, he looked at the paper with tears forming in his eyes. He then blurted out, "You know what, I don't want to go here anymore."

He let his academic schedule fall to the floor, got up from his chair, grabbed his belongings, and walked out with his mother. It felt as if everything was happening in slow motion. The academic advisor looked puzzled and confused. She didn't see what had happened just before, and she looked to me and the rest of the orientation team to shine light on the situation. Because of the sensitive nature, we urged her to continue with the scheduled program and tend to the other waiting students.

Reader, you can only imagine how badly I wanted to jump in and intervene in this young man's dilemma. I could not believe what I had witnessed. It brings tears to my eyes, even now as I'm writing this and reliving that moment. Here we have a young man from Cleveland, Ohio, and not just any part of Cleveland. This kid is from the inner city, an area where it's extremely rare for a student to go to college. This young man has completed his Free Application for Federal Student Aid (FAFSA), passed all five parts of the Ohio Graduation Test, taken the ACT and the SAT, and was then standing on the cusp of college enrollment. He has fulfilled every requirement to make it to this point, but because his mother was unsupportive of his college dream, he decided to give up on his goals.

I could have reassured him of his aspirations and highlighted what could be an amazing life decision so that he would stay and follow through with his plan but there would always remain one hurdle: his mother. There may be people in your life who will try to stop you from pursuing your dreams. It may be a girlfriend, a boyfriend, your mother or father, your extended family, etc. Whoever this is, you cannot sacrifice your education and future livelihood for them.

Please feel me when I say this: the people who are trying to deter you from your dream have already LIVED THEIR LIVES! I'm not trying to judge anybody. All I'm saying is they have already lived their own lives and made their own decisions. Whether they went to college, picked up a trade, or started a family, they have already made their life decisions and decided how their lives will be. Don't sacrifice your dreams, your education, and your passion for anybody! You decide on your path and live your truth as the person you wish to become. It is now your turn to live your life the way you want to live it. There is a big world out there, waiting for you to come and be a part of it.

There are many people who, as teenagers, are tasked with the duty of helping their parents around their home: babysitting, paying bills, and completing house work. So they decide to stay home and continue to work at minimum-wage positions. Personally, I have nothing against working at fast-food joints and retail shops, but they often only pay minimum wage. Let me tell you something about a minimum-wage position. I don't care how many hours you work, it will NEVER pay you enough to support the decent lifestyle of a single, fully independent person. It surely will never help you support any family that you are sacrificing your dreams for. IT WILL NEVER DO IT! You can work seven days a week, eight to ten hours a day. It will still never do it! A minimum-wage job won't pay for the kind of lifestyle you want. This is why education is important. An education will change the **quality** of your life, if you let it. Now beware, I didn't say it would make you rich, but it will indeed change the quality of your life if you allow it to.

I'll never forget my first real minimum-wage job. I was working at a daycare in Cleveland. Minimum wage at that time was $7.30 an hour. I was in high school at the time, so I could only work part time. My paychecks averaged about $166.65 every two weeks. This was a decent amount of money when I was only focused on taking care of myself. But my mother often needed help with covering bills. One week, she may have needed $100; the next week, she may have needed $60. In the end, this added up, and I often wasn't even left with enough money for the bus to and from work. Once I finished my bachelor's degree, I got a taste of what it felt like to work for two weeks and earn $1,000. Then, when my mother would call and ask for $100, I could give her $200 and still live my life without financial hardship. I was then able to go into Applebee's and say, "Hang on to that '2 for $20' menu—let me see what that full rack of ribs is about!" These may seem like small achievements to someone who was born of greater privilege, but to me it was a true highlight.

Student-to-Student Tip #2:

Never miss your first day of classes!

Before classes start in the fall, there are typically lots of parties and celebrations taking place on and off campus. Some of those parties and celebrations are thrown by the school; others are thrown by student organizations. If you know you're going to be out late on Sunday before that first Monday morning class, be sure to get you're a$$ up in the morning.

Never miss your first day of classes! This day is the best opportunity to size up your professors. You will find out whether they are extremely strict or laid back. You will also receive your class syllabi on the first day, with an overview of what your professors expect from you academically the entire semester. They will let you know whether you need to purchase the textbook for the class, and they will review their attendance and extra credit policies. In many cases, they let you leave that first class early, so why not attend?

Here is an even more important thought: some professors will dive right into the class material on the first day. This is an even bigger reason to attend your first class! You wouldn't want to start the semester behind for no good reason, right? In short, don't miss the first class.

A Time to Reflect

1. What are your thoughts on making sacrifices while in college?

2. In what areas of your daily life do you believe you will need to make sacrifices? Are they similar to those discussed in the chapter?

3. Think about any potential family or friends you may need to sacrifice to ensure your success. Do any in particular come to mind?

4. Reflect on the Cleveland student's college orientation experience with his parent. How did this situation make you feel? Did you agree with the parent? Why do you think the parent reacted the way she did to her child leaving for college?

5. It was said a higher education has the power to change the quality of your life. What do you think is meant by this?

Scholarship Hunt Tip #2:

Check with your parents places of work. You would be surprised how many students find scholarships from their parents employers. For me personally I struck out in this area. I once had a student tell me he found a $2,500.00 scholarship, at his dads' place of work which was renewable for 4 years as long as he maintained a 3.0 GPA. Beware, some of these scholarships often have grade point average requirements, extracurricular preferences, and some may be major based. All-in-all, leave no scholarship or grant unexplored.

CHAPTER 3

Control Your Inner Hater

GOING TO COLLEGE is a challenge in itself. How do people keep their positive energy flowing to stay motivated in school? Well, the third secret to surviving college involves controlling your self-doubt. I always say there are two different influences in your head. I like to call these voices your "inner hater" and your "inner motivator." Picture having the positive angel and negative devil floating over your shoulders.

Your inner motivator/hater trying to persuade you

Both of these little voices feed off your outlook on life. The more you talk and think about failing at something, the more the guy in the red (your inner hater) will convince you that there is no coming back from your letdown. The more you talk and participate in successes, the more the guy in the white (your inner motivator) will encourage you to continue on that successful path.

Now, you may be thinking that you rarely ever hear your inner motivator speak to you. This may be true—in some cases, we rarely hear our inner motivator speaking to us because it is starving! Remember that we feed these little voices by what we say and do.

If you rarely say anything positive or rarely act on your positive thoughts, your inner motivator will starve. Then your inner hater takes over because you have not achieved anything positive. Your inner hater is also an ass. It loves to kick you when you are down. I can give you an example from my high school days. Back then, I was one of the best students academically. I graduated from high school with a 4.0 cumulative GPA. At that time, the state of Ohio issued a mandated standardized test, the Ohio Graduation Test (OGT), that all sophomore students had to complete. This test had five parts—math, science, history, reading, and writing—and students must pass all five areas before they can graduate from high school. I thought, being an academic high achiever, that I would pass the test with no problem. I remember taking the OGT for the first time and walking away confident that I had passed all five parts. Sometime later that year, our homeroom teachers shared our test results with us. Some students were jumping for joy, elated to have passed all five OGT exams . . . and then there were those of us who could only sit with this expression:

Me salty AF that I didn't pass all five parts

I felt like this because I had failed one of the exams. I tried playing it off like it was no big deal, but on the inside, I was deeply embarrassed. I couldn't understand what the hell had happened. I had a perfect GPA! How could this happen to me?! I knew students who slept through their classes but had passed all five parts. I kept thinking something had to be wrong. I failed the history portion of the test, and at that time, one of the voices in my head began to speak. My inner hater heard my distress signal and began to tear me down piece by piece. "What a dummy. You thought you were so smart! NOPE, you're a dumb a$$. Looks like you won't be graduating from high school. And you thought you could go to college!" When I got home, my ego was bruised, and I was still in disbelief. My friends were happy: they had passed all five parts, even though my GPA was higher than theirs. I needed some time alone to collect my thoughts.

A quick tip: it's always good to take a step back and think things through carefully when you're upset. If you don't, you may end up doing something you will regret. Personally, I wanted to lash out at people who had nothing to do with my failure. But instead, I took some time to reflect on what had happened, and I heard my inner motivator begin to speak. That voice told me to find a teacher who could help me pass the history OGT the next year.

I sought out my ninth-grade history teacher and bluntly told him that I had failed the history OGT test and needed something to study over the summer. He gave me two pieces of study material: a book that focused on the history facts that commonly show up on the test and a set of history flash cards. That summer, I developed my plan of attack for the OGT history test. I wasn't a big fan of reading, especially during the summer. So I made a plan to read just two pages per night from the book he gave me and to study just two flash cards each night. On Fridays, I would test myself to see what I remembered. This worked out perfectly, because I didn't feel like I was missing out on anything during the summer, but I was also training and preparing for my final OGT.

My eleventh grade year, I took my history OGT again, and this time I passed. I won't sit here and tell you that I passed the test with flying colors or that confetti fell from the sky, because that isn't what happened. I barely passed, but it was good enough. At that time, I didn't hear my inner hater much. That piece of $%!+ rarely has anything to say when you're winning!

Once I passed that hurdle in my life, I decided I was ready to start looking into colleges. Before I knew it, I was battling with the SATs and the ACTs. When I took my ACT for the first time, I scored 14 out of 36! This was terrible. You can't get into most colleges with an ACT score of 14.

Me crying again, "WORLD WHY DO YOU HATE ME!?

Again, I was baffled by the fact that I was a straight A student who kept performing poorly on state and national standardized tests. On the verge of giving up, I wasn't sure what to do. I started thinking that maybe college wasn't for me. Maybe I should stop trying to go. Maybe this was a sign from above. Right when my spirits were getting low, my inner hater decided to show up and go in for the kill. "First the OGT, and now this? 4.0 my @#$! You might as well stop now and get your application in at the fast food restaurant down the street. The college dream is over for you!" A part of me really believed that voice. Here I was again, failing at something when I thought I should have succeeded. Some of my friends and peers had earned much better scores, at least college admittance level, and I was left feeling stupid. I wasn't sure what move to make next. But, after taking a moment to calm down and reflect, I heard my inner motivator start whispering to me. He told me that I should study and take the test again; maybe I could get a higher score. I took my own advice, studied, and took the test again. This time, I received a 17. Now, this score isn't great, especially not for a 4.0 student, but it wouldn't prevent me from being admitted into a decent college. When I received my first college acceptance letter, I could have cried. At that point, I'd faced so many hurdles that could have prevented me from achieving my goals, yet I could FINALLY say I'd made it!

I share my personal testimony with you to say this: your inner hater is a vicious son of a . ..... well, you get the point. That voice will push you to quit when you know deep down that you ought to keep trying. That voice has the persistence and energy to overpower your dream of success, but only if you let it. Please watch what you say to yourself and what thoughts you allow to enter your mental space, because those words and thoughts can drive your actions. I never would have thought, with all of these academic setbacks, that I would go on to receive two associate degrees, a bachelor's degree, and a master's degree. But, before I could move past my challenges in high school, I had to gain control over those two voices in my head. Some of you reading this book may not believe that the inner hater and the inner motivator are real. If you ever want to test the power of the two, pay attention to how you feel when you experience any hardship. Think about what your thoughts tell you. Reflect on whether you are continuously positive or if you tend to shy away from your goals because of self-doubt.

Student-to-Student Tip #3:

If you are not a morning person, avoid morning classes!

If you know that you are not a morning person, but you decide to schedule early morning classes anyway, your inner hater will voice its opinions loud and clear as you're sleeping. When you are in a deep sleep and your inner hater starts talking about attending class, it typically goes like this: "Stay in bed! Don't worry about that class today. Just get the notes from your classmates tomorrow. It's only one day."

Don't listen to this voice. The easiest way to do that is to avoid early morning classes if you aren't naturally a morning person.

<u>**A Time to Reflect**</u>

1. What do you think about the idea of "the inner hater and the inner motivator" concept within this chapter. Do you believe they exist?

2. Think of a time when your inner hater made you doubt yourself?

3. Think of a time when your inner motivator helped motivate you?

4. Between your inner hater and inner motivator, which of the two do you think have more power over you? Why?

Scholarship Hunt Tip #3:

Check with your family bank. Many perspective college students don't know banks, large and small, are often eager to contribute to student's post-secondary education. I actually picked this up when I was in college working as an admission counselor. During a presentation on campus, I shared this scholarship hunting tip with one of my families from Cincinnati, OH. Not long after the student reached out to me and shared the news that his bank gave him a $10,000 scholarship, that would be awarded over four years. That scholarship, coupled with other university merit-based scholarships, made it possible for this student to attend college for very little money out of pocket!

CHAPTER 4

Get Some Positive Friends

THE FOURTH SECRET to surviving in college is to get some positive friends. These are friends who spend the majority of their time listening to their inner motivators. These students are concerned with being successful and with creating a balance between the college party scene and the academic world. Finding a group of friends like this can be difficult, especially if you don't already know anyone who's attending your college. I think the best place to start your search is within the classroom. Personally, when I started college, I didn't know that having a positive group of friends really mattered. Actually, I thought college was supposed to be this big party, where you're always drinking and partaking in other adult activities. (Ha!)

Now, I won't sit here and tell you that I didn't go out and enjoy myself in college. I actually had a great time. But the key is finding a group of friends who know how to succeed and how to create that balance between partying and studying.

When I was a tour guide for my college, every tour would have a couple of students who would ask the questions everybody wanted to know but didn't want to ask in front of their parents: "What are the parties like at this school? Are they lit? Are they turnt?" This student was focused on how exciting our party culture was, or was not. My response was probably not the one they expected. Yes, I told students that we had MANY parties, and there was something different for each person, but I heavily stressed the importance of creating a balance between work and fun with the prospective students. I explained that there are three different types of students.

First, you have your party animal.

THE PARTY DONT START 'TILL I WALK IN

Your standard university party animal will tell you that this university is the perfect place to turn up and have a great time. Some of these party animals begin college and barely attend classes for their entire first month while going to every party. These students often end up on academic probation or suspended for poor academic performance. True party animals have no time for classes or for sleep!

Secondly, you have the bookworm.

CAMPUS POLICE!?

THEY KEEP DISTURBING MY STUDIES

DON'T DISTURB THE BOOK WORM!

The bookworm student is extremely invested in his or her studies and nothing else. Bookworms don't care much about making friends. They don't care about going out to enjoy the college experience. Bookworms are solely focused on getting their degrees and moving on to the next phase in their lives. When you ask bookworms about the party scene in college, they are probably going to look at you like you are crazy. They might even say something like, "Parties? We don't party much here."

These students may miss out on the college party experience, but they won't be getting kicked out of school for poor academic achievement. I'd pick the bookworm's position over the party animal's any day.

Finally, there is the student of balance.

WHEN BEING THE GOAT ALL IS POSSIBLE!

This student knows how to enjoy the party scene in college but still achieves high academic marks. THIS IS THE KIND OF STUDENT I WANT YOU TO BE. I don't want you to do so much partying that your academic performance suffers. I also don't want you to be the student who misses out on the once-in-a-lifetime opportunities to enjoy college because you're so focused on the next phase of your life. Why rush so blindly through college that you miss out on the opportunity to meet great people who could possibly open new doors for you?

You also want to keep a positive group of friends who can assist you with studying, having a social life, and finding job or internship opportunities. Sometimes you can get all these friends to be in the same circle with you, and sometimes it doesn't work out that way. This is okay. If you have various circles of friends that each make you feel fulfilled in a different way, this is okay as well.

For me personally, I didn't have a large circle of positive friends going into college. I had four friends from Cleveland who attended college with me. We helped each other complete assignments and study for exams, and we were there for each other when we needed emotional or social support. Having a positive group of friends—even a small group—helps create that balance you need to stay mentally and emotionally stable throughout your college years. Keep some positive friends. Friends on the positive spectrum can be lifesavers, while those on the negative side can sink you like a ship.

<u>Student-to-Student Tip #4:</u>

Don't party too hard on Sunday night

It will affect your Monday morning! I generally used Sunday nights for personal grooming and homework. Partying hard extremely late into Saturday night will give you a late start on Sunday; you may even spend the entire day trying to drag yourself out of bed. When you spend half of your day sleeping and recuperating from the previous night, you miss out on valuable study and personal organization time. Doing this again on Sunday night can mean a crappy Monday, and in some cases, a whole crappy week.

<u>A Time to Reflect</u>

1. Of the three a types of students described - party animal, bookworm, and the student of balance - which one do you think you identify most with? .... Be Honest!

2. How do you think your choice of friends will impact or hinder your success?

3. What are your thoughts on balancing academics and a social life?

Scholarship Hunt Tip #4:

Check for scholarships given out by your local community pillars, both for-profit and nonprofit. These will include your local sports teams, big businesses, foundations, churches, and your local clubs. These community pillars may also include local Greek-Letter Organizations. Leave no stone overturned when it comes to searching for support in your academic pursuits.

CHAPTER 5

The Power of the GPA

THE GPA: IT'S a number with huge meaning. Your GPA holds so much value when it comes to college admission, obtaining scholarships, and acquiring special academic honors. Secret number five to surviving college is all about your GPA.

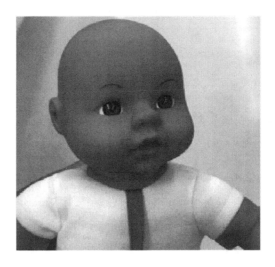

**Your GPA is your baby; the better you take care
of it, the better it will take care of you**

In chapter 3, I discussed my pre-college challenges, including my below-ideal ACT score of 17. While my ACT score was clearly not the highest, my 4.0 GPA made all the difference. So why did my ACT score not match my GPA? The answer is complex. I was born and raised on the lower east side of Cleveland, in what was historically known as Longwood. This area is now named Arbor Park and is a part of the Cuyahoga Metropolitan Housing Authority—in other words, public housing. For those who do not know, public housing is often known as "the hood" or "the projects." Because my public school was surrounded by several different public housing projects, there wasn't much tax funding from the community. Therefore, there was less monetary investment in the schools in my area. In addition to less-than-ideal funding, many students there were dealing with their own trying realities outside of school, which was often reflected in their behavior.

As my GPA reflected, I did everything required to excel in my public school classes. The problem wasn't how hard I worked but that the school didn't have the resources or sufficient tools to fully teach me the in-depth material that would make me competitive with my peers from better-funded schools. Subsequently, my knowledge of math and science was not ideally developed. It's also important to note. That I took little advantage of the opportunities that could have helped me get a higher test score. For example, when the guidance office would inform us about opportunities to take the ACT/SAT practice test or attend sessions that can help us improve our scores, I was always too busy. In other words, I wasn't interested in making time for that help or support. A quick tip, *take advantage of those opportunities to increase your test score.* Most colleges are giving out Merit bases scholarships based on GPA's and Test scores. For many of these scholarships, as long as you meet the criteria the scholarship is automatically yours. The scholarship grid below is a reference from a scholarship offered from an Ohio college in 2018.

2018 DIRECT FROM HIGH SCHOOL MERIT SCHOLARSHIP MATRIX							
Best University in Ohio logo was here!	ACT / NEW SAT Score						
High School GPA	35+	34-33	32-31	30-29	28-26	25-23	22-20
	1560+	1550-1490	1480-1420	1410-1350	1340-1240	1230-1130	1120-1020
+3.80	$6,000	$6,000	$6,000	$6,000	$5,000	$5,000	$3,500
3.60 - 3.79	$6,000	$6,000	$6,000	$5,000	$5,000	$3,500	$3,500
3.40 - 3.59	$6,000	$6,000	$5,000	$5,000	$3,500	$3,500	$3,500
3.20 - 3.39	$5,000	$5,000	$5,000	$3,500	$3,500	$3,500	$3,500
3.00 - 3.19	$5,000	$5,000	$3,500	$3,500	$3,500	$3,500	$1,000
2.75 - 2.99	$5,000	$3,500	$3,500	$3,500	$3,500	$1,000	$1,000

This is the kind of money you can receive just for doing what you are supposed to in school. Its automatic, you don't have to apply if you meet the criteria, its yours! In other words take care of your #$%&@#^ business in school!

In short, while I didn't perform well on standardized college entrance exams, my great GPA saved me, giving me the opportunity to attend college. Never underestimate the power of your GPA. Your GPA also goes a long way when applying for scholarships and sometimes even job opportunities. I have two interesting stories directly from my experiences about the power of the GPA.

During my second year of college, I was on a mission to recover my GPA. As I discussed earlier, I changed my major from pharmacy after my freshman year, realizing that I was neither passionate about nor good at pharmaceutical science. Because I lacked passion and skill in that area, my GPA took a huge hit. My GPA baby looked something like this:

My GPA baby after my freshman year of college

When the time came to change my major, my low GPA almost prevented me from getting into the education major I'd decided on. Luckily, I'd done just well enough to be accepted into the education program. I remember being on campus one day and stumbling across a flyer. A company that worked with the college of business was offering a $5,000 scholarship along with a $15 an hour job opportunity! Minimum wage at this time was $7.50. When I saw this opportunity, I was pumped, as any college student would be! I was ready to get paid until I read the bottom of the flyer. It said they were only looking for students majoring in business.

Needless to say, I was sad that I couldn't pursue the opportunity, but I decided to pass the news along to a friend who was a business major. This friend was in his third year at the university. I remember meeting up with him in the campus student union to share the flyer. I showed him the awesome job opportunity I'd found and asked whether he was still studying business. He said he was and took the flyer. At first, I could tell he was really excited. But his excitement didn't last long; his smile gradually faded. I remember I asked him what was wrong, and he took a long pause before replying. He showed me that they were looking for students who had a GPA of 2.5 or better. My friend, who was in his third year of college, had just a 2.3 GPA. At that moment, I could only imagine how he felt. It almost seemed like the flyer had spontaneously burst into flames. The craziest part of this situation was that the flyer stayed in circulation for a long time—the position could not be filled due to a lack of qualified applicants.

While I felt bad for my friend, I wasn't surprised, because I knew what kind of student he was. This friend was the kind of guy who spent more time partying than he did focusing on academics. He was the kind of guy who was okay with getting by in class with a C or D average, but those grades don't make you stand out as a student.

I always tell students: if you don't want what the average student has, then you must be willing to do what the average student won't! Think about that for a second. In this game of academia, the average students don't get high levels of recognition. You must be extraordinary in your efforts to become someone worthy of great opportunities. It's like seeing someone with the perfect physique at the gym and thinking to yourself, "I want a body like that." Well, that perfect body didn't just wish itself into existence. If you want that body, you've got to work for it. You can't get killer six-pack abs by eating three donuts a day and occasionally doing two sit-ups. You have to work hard. You have to do extraordinary work. The moral of this story is this: if you want something, you must be willing to put in the work to get it. If you want great opportunities throughout your college career, you must take care of your GPA!

On the flip side, I had a different friend whose extraordinary effort paid off in a major way for him. This friend was an engineering student and also in his third year of college. He took great care of his GPA, keeping a 3.5 cumulative average. Because of his extraordinary efforts, the college of engineering offered him an engineering co-op working out of state that summer. Through this opportunity, he earned $27 per hour–plus free housing–before he even graduated.

Don't underestimate the power of that GPA. I don't mean to encourage my readers to solely focus on the number of their GPA.

Your true focus should be on learning the content in your classes. If you've followed my above-mentioned advice, and if you focus on learning the material in a field relevant to you, your overall GPA will be in a great place. This will put you in an ideal position to take advantage of future opportunities.

Student-to-Student Tip #5:

Manage your college social credit score

Your GPA, other students' perceptions of you, and the faculty and staff's perceptions of you make up your college social credit score. These three areas combine to determine what enrichment opportunities you will receive on campus. If your GPA is strong, and both students and faculty can say nothing but great things about you, this will help you gain a world of new experiences. If you damage one of those areas, the opposite is true. For example, if your GPA is strong, and the students think you're awesome, but the faculty and staff don't have a high opinion of you, you could miss out. Keep all three of these areas in the positive and you should be on track for success and opportunity.

Also, very important for you to know. Consider this next advice as extra credit! There are two types of students in class: There is one that's there to **GET ATTENTION,** and one that's there to **PAY ATTENTION**... (I know that was deep right!? ☺) Figure out which one you are going to be!

<u>**A Time to Reflect**</u>

1. Where does your GPA currently stand?

2. What actions lead you to your current GPA? Where do you see you GPA in the future? How will you achieve this future GPA?

3. What are your thoughts on a social credit score in college?

4. Imagine that you have that same social credit score in high school, how are you performing in all three categories? Be Honest!

Scholarship Hunt Tip #5:

Check with the places you and your family eat at on the day to day basis. A lot of your local fast food restaurants offer scholarships. Your local grocery stores may offer scholarships,. If you have a family that spends a lot of time doing home repair, check with the big home repair companies. For many of these scholarships, you can check online by googling "scholarships offered by..." Happy hunting!

CHAPTER 6

Adjust Your Mind-Set

GOING TO COLLEGE is a really big transition. Many times, you will have to step back and evaluate whether your mental state is where it needs to be to ensure your success in college. The sixth secret to surviving college is to prepare your mind for the transitions to come. This isn't something that's normally talked about in classrooms or in movies that you may see, but your mental state is a critical factor in your college experience. You may be a high school student who is preparing to launch into your college journey, or you may already be a college student who's trying to figure out how to be more successful. Either way, this chapter will help you. If you're an incoming college freshman, it's especially important that you pay close attention. At this point in your life, you probably can't wait to get away from home. You may have been dreaming of the day when you can tell your family to "suck it" as you run out the door to the college of your dreams. For some of us, this transition may be easy; for others, it may be difficult. Either way, you need to prepare mentally.

For this part of the chapter, I want you to imagine something with me. Can you do that? Great! Move your phone away from you so there are no distractions.

Stop reading and do it! I'll wait.

Now that we've got that out of the way, I want you to imagine waking up on campus move-in day. Your outfit for your first day as a college student has been laid out for two weeks, there isn't one wrinkle or stain on it, and you have everything you need to be the grown-up college student you've dreamed of being for the last year. You and your family pack up your bags in the car and hit the road. Your parents are excited and happy for you, and you're happy too. But for some reason, you're not talking much in the backseat. You have your headphones on, quietly listening to your music. You're excited about school, but you're nervous too, all at the same time. When you arrive on campus, it's a beautiful day!

The birds are chirping and students are running around laughing and having a good time. Your parents, on the other hand, don't know how to act. They're saying things like, "Oh, this campus is beautiful! I can't wait to see your room! Look at these buildings! Wow, you are going to have such a great time in school! Let's go have lunch in the student union!" But as the day starts to wind down, you start to see your parents making faces like this:

Your parents expressing that they are ready to go

They will also start saying things like, "Well, you know we have to get back on the road. Your little brother has that thing going on at school tomorrow." You give them that one final hug goodbye, watch them hop in the car, and pull off without you. At this time, you may feel some type of emotional rush happening inside of you. You may have a lot of unanswered questions circling in your mind. You may be thinking:

- Man, I'm not going to see my parents every day like I always have.

- A couple of my friends who said they were coming to school here aren't anymore.

- I don't even know anyone at this school!

- Man, I'm not sure if I even want to do this.

If you find yourself questioning your new situation and feel your emotions rising, find a quiet space on campus where nobody will judge you and let those emotions run free. I'll repeat this again: I need you to find a private space on campus where NOBODY can judge you and let your emotions run free. This could mean anything. It could mean screaming at the top of your lungs or punching at the air. (Please don't punch an actual person, because that would get you kicked out of college fast!) You might need to let a few tears fall. Do whatever you need to do to help you accept that your life is about to transition into a new phase, setting you off onto an unknown path. I always feel that journey all over again when I talk about the college transition. You can go ahead and pick your phone back up now. Thanks for putting that away for our journey. I know you are ready to make sacrifices.

Now why did I take you on that journey? Every year, all across this country, students head off to colleges and universities. They pack up everything they need, pens, pencils, clothes, and all their necessary materials for college. In the mist of all their gathering most students forget to deal with the emotions that accompany the fact that their worlds are changing forever.

Not every student will need to take that moment of reflection. Some students will be okay emotionally, immediately ready to wave goodbye to their parents and start exploring their new surroundings. But some of us genuinely need that moment of peace and reflection. Those who needed that time but didn't take it will usually experience a lockup period. If you go through this lockup, you won't feel ready to meet new people, resulting in you not wanting to stick around campus. Take the time you need to keep yourself emotionally stable and you will thrive throughout your college career.

<u>Student to Student Tip #6:</u>

You have to Mentally leave for college

Leaving mentally for college is a lot easier said than done. To help with the transition, it's always a good idea to attend your future colleges open houses and get to know other students that are also planning to attend in the future. Building these relationships with other future college students will help you become more comfortable with the transition. You can also start building relationships with the faculty that work at that institution. Faculty that have been working at that University for a while make great mentors!

A Time to Reflect

1. How do you feel about leaving for college? Are you excited or nervous? Why?

2. How do you intend to deal with your mounting emotions as you begin your journey into college life?

3. In your reflection period, what are some of the things you will think about?

4. How do you think your parents/siblings will respond on the day you actually move into campus?

<u>**Scholarship Hunt Tip #6:**</u>

Check for scholarship within companies that focus on the major you're interested in pursuing. For example let's say that you are interested in nursing. You should check with every company surrounding your area that interacts with the nursing profession. Check with local hospitals, local Nursing home facilities, and even a pharmacies. Hell, it would not hurt to check with any company that deals with the allied health and clinical profession. In the process of your search, you might meet a director in one of these companies that can help you throughout your college journey financially with scholarships. Or they can assist you by being one of your mentors. Imagine when it's time for you to do clinical work in your 3rd year of college, this person might be able to help you in securing space for your rotations or even a career at their company upon your graduation. Relationships reader, build relationships!

CHAPTER 7

Take No Losses!

SECRET NUMBER SEVEN to surviving college is adopting the philosophy that in life we only take in wins and lessons–NEVER losses. It took me a while to understand this principle, but it makes so much sense. When you remove the possibility of losing at anything, you can never lose. Having the view that you are either winning or learning keeps you motivated to push forward.

I might have stopped pushing forward back in high school if I had viewed my academic setbacks as losses. Don't get me wrong; I know there will be things that happen in your life and during your education that will scream FAILURE. But it's ultimately up to you to dig deep within and find the lesson to be learned from that situation. Once you've found the lesson and learned from it, you have turned a potential loss into a win. For example, before starting college, I wanted to be a pharmacist. I believed that I was going to be a pharmacist because I had done well in my high school math and science classes. My very first college chemistry class showed me that I lacked the proper background and in-depth knowledge to survive a rigorous program of math and science. Instead of seeing this misfire as a loss, I changed my perspective on it and realized it was an eye-opening lesson. I was not passionate about pharmacy, and I obviously was not good at the foundational skills I would need to succeed in it. Once I started to see my setback as a lesson, I came to believe that being scared half to death in that chemistry class on the first day of my college career was one of the best things to ever happen in my journey.

Your mind-set about your wins, losses, and lessons in life will affect how successful you are in every pursuit. Never underestimate the power of your thoughts. At the same time, framing your mind to think like a winner is only half the battle. You must be willing to also take action to become a winner. You know, once you've talked the talk, you've still got to walk the walk!

Let me clarify. You can't just say, "I'm a winner because I always think like a winner." You have to put winning actions behind your winning mentality. For example, if you're in your senior year of high school now and you're thinking, "I'm going to college," congratulations, you have a winning mentality. But if you haven't yet researched any colleges or scheduled any campus visits, then your actions aren't on the same page as your thoughts. Both your thoughts and your actions should be moving you in the same direction: toward your success. As another example, if you are currently a college student, you may say you want to finish the semester with a GPA higher than a 2.5. If, however, you only study the bare minimum to slide by in each class, your actions do not match your mentality.

Many times the talk-without-action scenario occurs when you face the fear factor of losing. The fear of losing and fear of the unknown are tremendous hurdles to overcome. Please note that working toward a no-losses mentality may sometimes bring discomfort into your life. You may not feel comfortable trying new things, or you may feel uncomfortable changing your mind-set in a new environment. Embrace this discomfort—it will help you grow and become stronger.

Take no losses with your friends, either. Sometimes, as you start to see your life from an angle of wins and lessons but no losses, you'll realize that you've outgrown some of the people around you. I once met an honor student who became very depressed about leaving for college. His teachers and his mother noticed that something was wrong and asked if I could speak with him. I asked him what was going on. He explained that he didn't want to leave his block or the familiar neighborhood because his close friends weren't planning on going to college with him. One friend told him that he wasn't going to college because he was tired of school and he would rather continue "hustling" for a living. When he told me this, I gave him this face.

I had to explain to this young man that everyone around him would not share his same dreams and aspirations. I let him know that he was leaving to better himself, and sometimes friends can be lost simply by the distance but he would make new, long-lasting friendships. These friendships will often fill that void of drifting apart from friends that you were once close to back home.

Understand that all of your friends aren't going to travel the same path as you. This may feel like a loss, but it's all about your mentality in this situation. You have a lot to gain from your new road ahead, and you cannot sacrifice those gains out of the fear of losing a friend. True friendship will transcend any move or new journey, if both parties are willing to keep in touch. Also be aware of your personal growth and changes. If you ever return home from college and old friends start to mention that you act different or sound different, you must be doing something right. Going to school is supposed to make you into a different person: an upgraded, better-rounded version of yourself. You are growing, and the people who aren't growing much will notice the changes faster than anyone else. The journey of postsecondary education is designed to be life-changing.

Now, of course, there will be things about you that will not change. Your core personality traits will always be the same. Myself, I have always been a silly guy—I can be a real jokester—and to this day, this has not changed. Not much of your core personality will change unless you have a habit hindering your success that you decide to change. Those changes all fall under your wins and your lessons. Don't be afraid to alter who you were to become great. Notice I didn't say to become "good" or "okay." I said don't be afraid to alter yourself to be GREAT!

So there you have it. Seven major tips to help you thrive during your college journey. If you follow these tips, I promise your journey will be much smoother than someone who only used this book as a table decoration. Use these words to help yourself stabilize in college and to become great. Remember, this journey isn't about going to college to be average. This is about going to college to become extraordinary. Develop the potential that your family, your community members, and your former teachers have seen in you. Visualize your plan for your future, and capitalize on it. You truly can do whatever you want in this world. The key is all mentality. As the saying goes, if you change your mentality, you will change your reality!

<u>Student to Student Tip #7:</u>

Find alternative ways to pay for expensive books

Books in college can become very expensive. So much so that you might want to walk in the store, grab one and run out the door with it! No please don't do that, it was just a joke. The lessons and skills you will receive from your entire college journey are much more valuable than stealing a book from the book store. That's why I recommend stealing 5 or more! Again just joking, please no stealing! If you happen to find yourself in a jam where you can't afford the text book, build a relationship with a friend in the class that you can share the book with. You can also talk to the professor and see if he/she has one on hold in the library for you to use throughout the semester. If you do have some money to purchase the book, I would recommend looking into renting text books or purchasing them online. They can be cheaper this way. **Again no stealing! It was just a joke!**

A Time to Reflect

1. Describe a time where you turned a loss into a lesson?

2. Within the chapter there was discussion about matching your words to your actions. Can you share an example of how your words are matching your actions?

3. What do you think of the idea of outgrowing some of your high school friends? How do you think this loss can be converted into a gain or lesson?

4. If you could send a message to the author (and you should), what would you say about this book?

5. Send your message to me directly on Instagram: Chrisscottmotivates. Email: Reachtoteachnational@ gmail.com

<u>Scholarship Hunt Tip #7:</u>

Check with your local library and all throughout the world wide web for scholarships. Many local libraries keep books on file that consist of scholarships available for the academic year. Aside from the library being a resource, the internet can be your best friend when looking for college scholarship dollars. This information is highly important to share because millions of dollars in scholarships get returned each year because students don't apply for them or students are missing the application deadlines! You will want to circle this next sentence The juicy window of opportunity for scholarship applications normally occurs between October 1st and runs until the end of March. Apply! Apply! Apply!

GOOD LUCK!!

Questions to ask during a college visit:

Academics

What programs are popular at this institution?

Does your school offer... (What you are interested in studying)

What is the average class size of introductory classes?

Do you have an honors college?

Do you have learning communities for freshman?

Where are the best places to study on campus?

Financial Aid

What percentage of financial need does the school typically meet?

What is the average merit award?

What other scholarship opportunities does your institution offer?

What is the average college debt that students leave with?

What type of work-study opportunities do you have?

What is your advice on loans?

Graduating Students

What is your four-year graduation rate?

What is your five-year graduation rate?

What does it take to graduate in four years?

What percentage of freshmen return for sophomore year?

Academic Support

What type of tutoring programs you have for incoming students?

What kind of learning disability resources do you have?

Does your institution have success coaches?

Is there free academic support or tutoring? Is it effective?

Are there social orientation programs for freshmen? Are they enjoyable?

Is there career counselling? Is it helpful?

Outside Campus Opportunities

What percentage of students get internships?

What percentage of students find careers after graduation?

What percentage of students study abroad?

What kind of career services do you have?

Where do students tend to hang out on and off campus?

Campus Living

How many residence halls (dorms) choices are there on this campus?

What is your total student population?

What percentage of students live on campus?

What is the process for roommate selection?

How many dining halls does your campus have?

Does the dining hall accommodate special dietary restrictions?

Does your institution have sororities and fraternities?

How ethnically diverse is the campus?

How many student organizations does your campus have?

What's the party scene like? (Probably best to ask current students)

What are some big campus events?

Is it easy to get around campus or get off campus without a car?

Can you bring a car to campus?

How do most students get around campus?

Is it safe to walk around at night? What kind of safety measures are in place?

Where would I go to find a part time job on campus?

Extracurricular

What are some of the most popular extracurricular and why?

What clubs or other opportunities exist for community service?

Do sports play a large role on campus? What division sports teams do you have? What about intramurals.

Does your campus have a recreation center? How often can students use it? Can we invite guest that don't attend this college?

Personal Questions (for presenter/tour guide)

What do you like most about this campus?

What do you like least about this campus?

Why did you pick this school?

What do you wish you would have known going into freshman year?

What do you wish you would have asked on a campus tour when you were in my place?

What surprised you about campus life here?

What would be your most important advice for freshman?

What's your favorite spot on campus?